My Sikh Community

Kate Taylor and Jasveer Kaur Deogan

Photography by Chris Fairclough

W

FRANKLIN WATTS
LONDON • SYDNEY

This edition 2007
©2005 Franklin Watts

First published in 2005 by
Franklin Watts
338 Euston Road
London NW1 3BH

Franklin Watts Australia
Level 17/207 Kent Street
Sydney, NSW 2000

ISBN: 978 0 7496 7371 0

A CIP catalogue record for this book
is available from the British Library

Printed in Malaysia
Planning and production by Discovery Books Limited
Editor: Laura Durman
Designer: Ian Winton

The author, packager and publisher would like to thank the following people for their
participation in this book:
   Bhai Sahib Bhai Mohinder Singh Ji
   Jasveer's family
   Jasveer's friends
   Manisha Raju
   Poonam Kartia
   Wilkes Green Junior School
   Head Teacher Mr. A. S. Mangat MBE BSc
   Miss Malhi
   DTF Book Shop
   Soho Supermarket
   Badial
   Onkar Eye Centre & Mr G. S. Changan BSc (hons) M C Optom.

Photo acknowledgements: Guru Nanak Nishkam Sewak Jatha (Birmingham) UK
pp. 19, 20 bottom, 23 top, 25 left, 27 top and bottom, 28.

Franklin Watts is a division of Hachette Children's Books.

Contents

All About Me

My name is Jasveer Kaur Deogan and I'm eight years old. I am a *Sikh*.

I live in Handsworth, in Birmingham. Lots of other Sikhs live here too.

▼ With my mum and dad in Handsworth.

I live in a house with my mum, my dad and my two sisters, Inderjeet who is 16 years old, and Naam who is 10. I share a bedroom with Naam. We have a bunk bed and my bed is on the top. There are stairs in our room that lead up to Inderjeet's room.

▲ **Me in my bedroom.**

My Family

I have a big family, and most of my relatives live in Handsworth too.

My mum was born in India but moved to England when she was four years old. She has five sisters and four brothers. Most of them live nearby, but two of her sisters still live in India.

▼ **This is my family.**

My dad is from Kenya. He moved to Birmingham when he was five years old and all of his family live here now. His brother lives in the same road as us.

All of my grandparents live in Handsworth and I see them almost every day. One of my grannies makes me pretty Indian clothes. She's really good at it!

▼ **Me with my grandparents.**

▲ **My aunt, uncle and cousins live just down the road.**

Where I Live

I love living in Handsworth. It's really busy and there's always something to do.

◀ I live in this road.

We are friends with all of our neighbours, and often share lifts to the Gurdwara, our temple. My mum is always chatting to the grown-ups in the street while I play with the children.

▶ My mum (right) talking to our neighbour.

I like going to the park with my dad and my sister. We usually go to the one next to the library. It's hidden from the street and it's quiet there. I like playing on the climbing frame.

◀ **Me and Naam at the park.**

Shops

There are lots of different shops in Handsworth, and you can buy all sorts of things.

We go to the shops in Soho Road. I like looking at all of the clothes they sell there. Sometimes my sisters and me have outfits made. You can choose the material you want and have a *salwar kameez* made. They have really pretty material with lots of different patterns.

The food shops are full of delicious things to eat. My mum buys all the ingredients she needs for cooking Indian food, like fresh herbs and spices.

Lots of the shopkeepers on Soho Road are Sikhs. Sometimes they speak to me in *Punjabi* - I like practising with them.

▶ **The Sikh *optician* in Soho Road.**

◀ **The bookshop in Soho Road.**

My School

My school is called Wilkes Green Junior and it's just around the corner from my house.

Naam goes to the same school as me.

My favourite subject is art because I like drawing and making things to take home.

▶ **My teacher, Miss Malhi, is really nice.**

I'm much quieter at school than I am at home. I spend most of my time with my best friends who are in the same class as me.

◀ **Some of my friends at school.**

We always eat English food at school for lunch. I like to take jam sandwiches on white bread.

▶ **Me eating lunch with my friend Poonam.**

At breaktime, I love to skip with my friends. We have a really big rope, and sometimes two or three of us try to skip at the same time. It's fun!

My Friends

I have lots of friends, but my best friends are Manisha and Poonam.

Manisha and Poonam also live in Handsworth. We play together after school.

▲ **Me with my friends Manisha (left) and Poonam (right).**

When my friends come to my house, we usually watch a video or play outside. There is an activity frame in the garden and we have a paddling pool during the summer. Sometimes mum lets us have water fights, which is really fun!

▲ Me playing in the garden with my friends.

◀ Me and Manisha.

Food

I am a *vegetarian*. I like lots of different foods, but I never eat meat.

My whole family are vegetarians. As a Sikh I believe all living things are God's creatures and should not be killed.

▼ **My family eating dinner together.**

My mum is a good cook and makes really nice Indian food. She cooks loads of tasty vegetable dishes, which we eat with *chapattis*. I like makki di roti, a yellow chapatti made of cornflour. Sometimes we have food like baked potatoes and pizza too.

▲ **My mum cooking *curry* and chapattis.**

My favourite foods are parathas (fried flat breads) stuffed with potatoes, and ice cream.

My Hobbies

I have plenty of hobbies, and I spend a lot of my spare time at the Gurdwara.

I go to gymnastics once a week at a church hall with my friend, Simarnpreet Kaur. It's brilliant.

▶ **Me doing gymnastics.**

I can do cartwheels but am still learning to do a handstand. It's really hard.

I like making things at home like cards and pictures. The other day I made a bag out of felt with a flower on it. It's really pretty.

◀ **I put lots of different things on my cards, like flowers, stickers and string.**

I love going to the Gurdwara because there's always something to do. We sing, pray and recite hymns out of the Guru Granth Sahib (the Sikh holy scriptures). Sometimes I help cook in the huge kitchen there too.

▼ **Me helping to make chapattis in the Gurdwara kitchen.**

Languages

I speak English most of the time but I'm also learning a language called Punjabi.

I have lessons every week at the Gurdwara where I learn to read, write and speak Punjabi. There are lots of posters in our street which are written in the language and I always try to read them.

▲ This festival banner is written in Punjabi and English.

◀ Me in my Punjabi class.

I practise speaking Punjabi with my grandad. Sometimes I find it difficult to remember the words though.

▲ **Me talking to my grandad in Punjabi.**

Clothes

I wear jeans and t-shirts at home but on special occasions I wear a salwar kameez.

A salwar kameez is a pair of trousers and a tunic. I sometimes wear a scarf, called a dupatta, to cover my head too.

▶ **Me with my sisters in our favourite salwar kameez.**

Sikh men always wear a *turban*, but my dad wears Western clothes most of the time. When he goes to the Gurdwara, he wears a special white outfit called kurta pyjama.

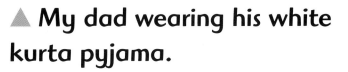

▲ **My dad wearing his white kurta pyjama.**

My mum always wears a salwar kameez at home. She wears Western clothes to work though.

◀ **My mum wearing a salwar kameez and a dupatta.**

Music

I normally listen to religious classical music, but I also like *Hindi* music.

At the Gurdwara I learn to sing religious hymns and to play the harmonium, a type of organ. It's a bit like the piano.

My dad plays the *tabla*. It's really difficult and takes a lot of practice. Sometimes he teaches us at home.

▼ **My dad plays the tabla while I play the harmonium.**

We also have a sitar, which is like a long guitar that sits on the floor.

▶ **This is a sitar.**

▲ This boy is showing how to play a sitar at the Gurdwara.

I like the music they play at the Gurdwara when we pray. Lots of people sit around playing instruments and singing. Sometimes everybody joins in and we sing shabads (hymns).

Religion

Being a Sikh is really important to me. I like praying and going to the Gurdwara.

Sikhs believe that ten gurus who lived a long time ago taught us that there is one God and showed us how to live an honest life.

▲ A picture of the ten gurus.

▲ These are my *prayer beads.*

Prayer is an important part of my religion. When we pray at the Gurdwara, we have to take our shoes off and cover our heads as a sign of respect to God.

I pray at home in the morning before school. Then I say an evening prayer called rehras with my whole family together.

▲ **A prayer meeting at the Gurdwara.**

▶ **Me praying with my family.**

27

Festivals

We celebrate lots of Sikh festivals in Handsworth. I really like Diwali and Vaisakhi.

During a festival, people put up banners all the way down Soho Road. I like putting on my Indian clothes and seeing everybody else dressed up too.

My favourite festival is Diwali. It celebrates the time when the sixth Guru, Guru Hargobind Sahib Ji, rescued 52 kings and princes from a prison in India. We let off fireworks from the roof of the Gurdwara at night, and light candles and lamps in our house.

◀ **Diwali fireworks.**

Vaisakhi is the Sikh New Year festival. It takes place in the Spring. We have lots of colourful celebrations in Handsworth. I go to the Gurdwara really early in the morning to pray with my family. It's a time for people to start a new life, and to stop doing bad things like lying. Lots of Sikhs want to be *baptised* during Vaisakhi.

▼ ▶ **Sikhs take part in a religious procession during Vaisakhi, called Nagar Kirtan.**

I like Birmingham

I like living in Birmingham. I used to live in Cardiff but I have lots of friends here now and am near my family. Also, our Gurdwara is around the corner and I love going there.

Glossary

Baptised When Sikhs are baptised, they become full members of the Sikh religion. They are called Khalsa, which means pure.

Chapatti A thin Indian bread.

Curry An Indian dish flavoured with spices and usually eaten with rice.

Gurdwara The building in which Sikhs worship. As well as a prayer hall, every Gurdwara has a kitchen and eating area, called a langar hall. Food is cooked by volunteers, and served, free of charge, all day. A lot of Gurdwaras also offer lessons at the weekend. These are often about the history of Sikhism. They also teach the Punjabi language.

Hindi Music that is sung in the Indian language called Hindi.

Optician A person who tests people's eyes, and who sells glasses and contact lenses.

Prayer beads A string of 108 beads or knots, sometimes called a 'mala'. People use prayer beads to help them pray.

Punjabi A language from the Punjab region of India and Pakistan.

Salwar kameez A pair of trousers and a loose tunic top.

Sikh A person who follows the Indian religion called Sikhism.

Tabla A set of two small drums, usually played in North Indian music.

Turban A headdress worn by Sikh men. It consists of a piece of cotton or silk that is wound around the head in a special way.

Vegetarian A person who does not eat any meat.

Index